# The Path of Difference

**Poems by Jamal Gabobe**

# The Path of Difference

**Poems by Jamal Gabobe**

REDSEA- REDSEA-ONLINE.COM Cultural Foundation
Ponte Invisibile Ed.
Fidiyaha Aqoonta iyo Ereyga Dhigan - Xarunta dhexe
Daarta Oriental Hotel - Hargeysa, Somaliland
Telephone: 00 252 2 525109 - Email: bookshop@redsea-online.com

Published by Ponte Invisibile (redsea-online), 2021, Hargeysa

Inquiries to the editor
Via Pietro Giordani 4, 56123 Pisa, Italy
www.ponteinvisibile.com
email: editor@redsea-online.com | editor@ponteinvisibile.com

ISBN 88-88934-72-3

EAN 9788888934723

CONTENTS

*Love never dies*

*If it dies, it wasn't love.*

# Pax Pacifica

Bone deep cold

touched by the sun rays

wakes up the body

reminds it of the possibilities,

in the body's thoughts

through the season of forgetfulness

Pacific breeze felt like the first time

slowly warming the senses.


The dialectics of hot and cold,

life and death,

after years vagabonding

bones crave their origin.

# Going Through It

Sleepwalking through life

days fold into each other,

can no longer tell

one from the next.

What I need is a clean break

but all breaks are dirty

simply 'cause they're breaks,

and no break is like another.


I realize at this demanding hour

can't say better late than never

cause timing is everything, as they say.

The monstrous hour approaching,

familiarity offers no protection.

I already see the end,

feel so unprepared.


Splintered images, dreams buried

but not forgotten.

They're here again

I tell myself to man up to the moment.

but how can I severe the hand feeding me

even if it's more of the same?

what can no longer be stomached.

# Doing & Un-doing

The night hunter navigating by instinct

in the jungle of dreams

it's late, maybe even too late

but that's neither here nor there

desire has a logic of its own.


What has to be done

should be done.

with care and devotion

it must be done.


What has to be un-done

must be un-done with heart and soul.


Doing and un-doing, made of the same stuff

deserve similar treatment.


Between the first day and last

when I set for the journey and now

so many doings, un-doings, too many details

the journey feels incomplete.

Driven off course, to deserted roads,

questionable spaces

where the seeds of rebellion are sown.

Distances widen between paper and pen

fugitive thoughts

no time for the tongue to speak itself

or quell the disorder, in a homeless heart.

A question pressing me

from so many directions

puts thought on edge

un-making what took so long to make.

What was there before

will it be there later,

the real thing,

or a mere shadow of its real self?

# Contraries

Fading strength, determination getting stronger

a clear mismatch that didn't last.

Later, it was the opposite.

Weakening determination, strength picking up

which was more debilitating.

Merely holding on is an achievement.

To dispossess, one must first possess.


At the crossing, the master showed no mastery,

the mystery was left unsolved.

At the moment when you looked so beaten

and all seemed lost, your fortunes revived.

The once bearable, now unbearable

nothingness, a moving target

to beat it at its own game, an unwinnable bet.

Condemned to try anyway,

you bear what you can, un-bear what you can't.


The hours shrinking into minutes, seconds,

parts that could be explained.

But what about the other parts

that can't be explained,

sums that don't up?

Days and nights

working against each other;

the pull and push of broken hopes.

Words that wouldn't form.

What I tried to achieve but couldn't.

It's happening, I confess before you ask,

so, you won't ask.

Doubts and hesitations own the moment

dissipating strength;

the once unbearable, now bearable.

The pain of ecstasy, long stretches of numbness,

days and nights spent at the mercy of contraries.

Banished emotions rally to the surface

pose for a photo. Smile. Click, click.

More of the same.

More or less.

More is less.

Less is more.

The sum less than the parts.

Absence and presence at each other's throat.

# The West and the Rest

They call us the rest.

They think they're being nice,

at their best.

But I have my doubts, about peaks and crests,

the west and the rest.

# Ordered Disorder

Messages coded, decoded, massaged ad infinitum

the order of things upset

day-to-day existence, or rather, subsistence

ordered disorder

until we find another way

or it finds us.

Something has to give.

Unlikely in the calculus of profit and loss

as gain and no pain

always soaring and never falling.

# Waiting to Be Fulfilled

The ghost of desire,

appearing out of nowhere,

wants to impose its sovereignty,

undermines it instead.


Inventing reasonable sounding justifications

that go against reason

twisting reality to align with it

gets its way temporarily

but remains unfulfilled.


It's not the first time this happens

and it won't be the last.

Desire never learns, it always wants;

even when it gets, it still wants,

enough is foreign to it,

always waiting to be fulfilled.

# Falling

Strong gusts of wind,

some leaves rustle on the branches, stay green;

others fall on the ground, dry up, wilt, or become mushy

depending on rain or no rain,

depending on how many times it was stepped on by pedestrians,

cars and trucks,

depending on where they fall.

Different-sized leaves falling from the same tree.

One is the size of a dollar-bill, some are bigger and a few are

smaller.


Falling at different speeds.

One doesn't want to wait at all,

goes straight down;

another lingers for as long as it could

showing off its colors, acrobatic skills.

A third zigzags its way down.


They're different once they touch the ground,

Some willingly join the wind, going with the flow,

some bundle together, refuse to move

from their new locale, others moved once but that was all.

One perched in the middle of the street,

takes the shape of a crown.

I hesitate when approaching them.

The way I hesitate to rush past the disabled man trying to cross

the street.

I don't want to hear the swish of the leaves when

I step on them.

I don't want to fall against my will, a leaf swept by the wind,

so, I stay awake and away.

I make no promises or commitments,

just float.

Avoid for as long as I can

the beckoning embraces

because I know what comes after.

Uneasy lies the rock,

hanging at the edge of the cliff,

its destiny already set:

gravity's victim.


Sinking to the bottom of the well,

no time for sadness or regret,

action trumps words,

leaving behind hype and hyperbole.


Truth revealed in movement,

in the agony of falling,

not in speech.

# Dream #1

I have dreamt of you and prayed for you.

I can't recall them all,

but here is some of what I've lived and remember.


Your golden heart,

gives of itself,

doesn't hold back,

makes me stop and wonder,

so much goodness

in one heart.


Your prayers,

a shower of faith

at a moment of doubt.


The depth of your eyes,

say so much,

more than words,

take me beyond myself,

to you.

I'm so grateful.

Last night,

your image flickered

through my eyes.

I rejoiced,

just because it was you

in front of me,

your presence

rioting in my flesh.


I was walking towards you

but I could not reach you.

I walked fast.

I walked slow.

The result was the same.

I could not reach you.

It wasn't that you were faster

or that I was slower

I just couldn't reach you.

The psychic toll

It wasn't about speed and distance

but the psychic toll was out of control.

# Dream #2

Last night I couldn't sleep.

I lay in bed for hours, got up,

walked back forth in the room

till I was tired. Went back to bed.

Lay there for a while.

No sleep.

realized what was happening:

I was fighting sleep to get some sleep.

# Dream #3

Slapped in the face by mad dog waves

pulling me down,

I push back, try to stay above

the sea's salty breath.


I was so happy when I saw you last.

I want to be always as happy as that.

Why is happiness so hard?


When you're away,

I feel part of me severed.

I want you to come back.

You don't have to bring back

gone glory, or to make promises,

just come, let's become.


You're a world.

I wish you were here.

You're more than a wish.

More than you.

You're a world.

Speak to me.

You don't have to dish.

I wish you were here.

You're my world.

I want more of you.

your scent,

your voice,

you.

The rising tide opens up vulnerabilities.

Plagued by doubt, uncertainty

I question myself

I want to know the reason

behind this foreign agitation

hitting my nerves.

I've dreamt of you so often.

Each time you were different,

neither a bridge, nor a footpath.

There was a chance for us

to be on the same path,

and for you to be different,

but that was not to be.

I got in the way.

You got in the way.

Life got in the way.

We're back to where we started.

I have dreamt of you so often

but every time it's different.

You say you're the same

but things aren't the same.

You say it's just a dream.

Things can be the same and different.

If nothing is the same, nothing is different.

Put an end to this dry spell, please.

Let me in.

Make me in your dream.

Be my home.

I'm tuned to your heart's whispers,

to the sun's scent on your neck.

Talk to me.

Let the words out of their prison

and juju their way to my ears.


I succumb to the temptation, the fleshiness of the flesh,

a fantastic delirium, then a sudden crash.

No regrets.

Will do it again in a heartbeat.


I'm excited, eager,

ready for friendship.


I'm alert, alive,

ready to commit.


I'm alert, alive,

ready for love.


I have dreamt of you so often,

every time it's different.

# Wanting But Not Seeking

With so many claims flying around,

tentativeness, caveats obscuring the core,

prompting us to dig harder, trying to see or touch

what's behind the veil,

we continue the search because

we know it's in the nature of doubt

to eventually un-do itself and reveal.


Stressful moments exposing strengths & weaknesses,

the exquisite façade of wanting but not seeking,

lacking laser focus, the single-minded dedication of ants,

the will of hungry beasts;

and so the pendulum swings back and forth:

physical pain, mental pressure,

an awful combo,

sapping the will.

# Time's Imperatives

The sun, bathing the world in light

making it feel lighter,

prompting the urge to go out there, into that visible space, and
claim it,

triggering the dismissive sigh and desiring glance, elemental
conflict of self and other, the shrinking of the space between sky
and earth.


Still time, and time still escapes.

Tomorrow is almost here and yesterday definitely gone

suspended between the raging fire and moon promise,

the asymmetry of beginning and end,

records, archives, history's soiled hands

witnessing against the truth,


I can't read the future or dwell on the past,

so, I stick with the present,

whether it makes sense or not.

# Linguistic Bias

Some words don't get a fair shake.

Take the words that begin with Re

Revise, redraw, rehabilitate, replace.

As soon as you hear re, you think something is being repeated,

Re-done, which takes away from the word's impact,

makes it second or third-hand.


Effortless is a tricky word.

It hides the history behind it.

Earth revolving around the sun

may seem effortless

but that doesn't mean it's true.

Effortless is a fraudulent word

pretends to reveal what it's concealing.

# Time Conflict

The present pounces on the past, mines and shapes it.

The past sneaks on the present, overshadows and directs it,

dispossesses it, turns it into an object.

The future, not fully formed,

Keeps its cards close to its chest

hints at other possibilities, beyond

predator or prey.

# Now & then

You love being at the center.

It's in your eyes, mouth, cheeks.

You love it so much,

you glow.

And as the splitting hour approaches,

late in the evening,

you wonder why bring a good thing to an end.

You think of this as arbitrary, unjustified termination

a betrayal of trust.

Anger builds at perceived injustice

And your inability to reverse it.

It was different the first time I saw you

and heard the soft power of your words.

You were the center of attention

back then, it didn't affect you. You stayed as you,

an invitation to everybody in the room, to reconsider,

be themselves.

I won't say sorry, my mistake, I put you on a pedestal

cause you do belong there.

What happened or happens between us is something else, won't

take away from your deserved place.

As I said, you belong high up there.

Nobody can take that away from you

but I don't have to keep idolizing you

just because you sit on a throne.

# Which Is You?

Anxiety multiplies, strengthens the chain tying new fears to old

ones,

known maladies to unknown ones,

the bonds linking us

to questionable claims, the known unknowns

sinister heart, angelic face

untenable arguments at an odd hour;

one reality superimposed on another

submission and defiance, tenderness and cruelty

a history of false interpretations.

Scenes follow one another,

pages from same life, yet different

former glory undermined, coarsened

a rogue state of being.

I remember you saying:

'because I'm afraid of the end

I'm asking now

so you won't say, you never asked.'

Another time, I heard you say:

'spent force

trapped in the present and wondering

what's ahead.'

I also heard you say:

'one life seems plenty

much happened, little matters.

quality rather than quantity.'

Which of these sayings should I believe?

Which is you?

# Yesterday and Today

Frantic efforts to avoid another dry spell

deflect and delay the inevitable,

the see-saw of opposites,

the chaotic mix of now and then

dissonance of sight and sound.

Yesterday, we were planning for the future ahead

the coming breakthroughs, an inviting future.

Today overwhelmed by arguing, disagreements,

excuses, the blame game

feeding the ravenous monster

easier than starving it.

The equation that hurts.


Yesterday, we were excited about the promised welcome

Now an awkward silence greets us.

# Contested Spaces

One life, multiple stops

driven by delusions of discovery

a leap into the unknown

self still unsettled

questioning expression on the face

so little happened

so much left to be done.

Suspended between exactness and approximation,

slices of time, resurrecting old beliefs

in a new guise, witness to the raging fire

unfulfilled promises

the stark look and feel of nothingness.


Bright spaces, shadows without depth

lines, curves, forming re-forming

reflections, dark corners, lights,

contested spaces, a carnival of opposites

motion in a frame.

The journey takes its toll,

grievances not settled, unpaid debts

the cumulative weighing on self

pushing it beyond itself

past the muddy waters of ungoverned emotions

and ecstatic pain,

urging it to find an anchor or be one.

# The Matter Is No Longer in My Hands

The signs don't look good,

I take a detour to avoid the bumps, the combustion

of unmet expectations, false dreams

worsening predicament,

dreams are not what they seem

neither are defeats.


Self – standing alone, looking for no place

keeping its own company

choice out of no choice

not like the easy flow of changing seasons

the doggish pursuit of recognition.


A seductive voice with tempting words

breathing life into suppressed rage.

No easy victories but inch-by-inch crawling

out of the dungeon of broken promise.


Unfolding scenarios, scene after scene, debris strewn on

broken earth adding to the weight of the past

thoughts and emotions mixed up, bewildered

nothing is what it seems.


Heedless of limits, conditions, I make a move

to turn the tables on the status quo,

bare the geometry of grief, the split within

difference and desire on the horizon

imposing their will.

The matter is no longer in my hands.

# The Path of Difference

Telescoping the moment, through the right angle

giving it history, power, assigning roles, winners and losers,

the unwritten rules of the game remain unwritten.

Threat of the dividing hour

hanging over us,

And we wonder why it's come to this?

Why happiness is so hard?

Every action points to inaction,

duty abdicating to doubt, pressing challenge of

the path of difference, how to restore movement

belief in a contested future.

# Still on the Prowl

Figuring out things

without a script to follow

the thin line that separates, getting thinner.

One more sign of an unraveling world.

Someone threw you a line

but you couldn't hang on to it

and it slipped your grasp

so you remain,

still figuring out things,

still on the prowl.


The situation itself imposes its own logic

prods you to act or abstain

but you can't leave it at that.

Other considerations rise

and they too must be taken into account,

and then others,

the circle widens,

the water gets muddier

scattering the elements of decision.

Life is what it is: up, down, repetitious routine

conflicts, reconciliation, whatever

all not even a drop in an indifferent ocean,

the ironclad course sweeping us

whether we fit or not.

# Close at Work

This feeling of being so close to the work, so utterly alone with it, is hard to explain.

Part of you wants to keep it that way.

Another part wants to put a quick end to it.

Mind says time to trade for lighter things.

Heart says it feels so good, it hurts.

Essence of cliché that art is suffering.


Throw one more log in the fire,

hear the cracking sound of disappearing stem,

flames and wood locked together, so close at work,

giving light and warmth.

# Illusion of Being

## I

Morning light slips through the glass window.

A sip of coffee, jam and butter toast,

an orderly start, and you think the day will continue

this way, but experience tells it may not be so.

The sequence is not always right.


Raising the issue, not dissolving it

in the union of opposites, or retreat to the bunker.

The matter still stands.

Measures taken, not measuring up,

the dilemma of what to claim, what to leave behind.

The gap has become a gaping hole that won't close, no matter

what.


Looking for a safe place, even a temporary home

from the whirr of the wheel, doubt and weakness

the circulation of blood and money,

deceptive glow of slogans.

## II

An alarm went through my head, a warning

at first, I tried to brush it away, ignore it,

but that didn't work.

The feeling stayed - reminder of

the ordeal ahead.

I read the sign of what was coming

the pending emotional rollercoaster

I had no strength for it, and for once,

I made the right decision, declined to take part.

The juncture at which things came to a head and we

knew we had to go our separate ways.

We found it's easier said than done.

So we kept the connection, delayed the split

Got closer than we started with

And we knew we couldn't be apart.

By chance we met, not by choice

As if an outside force took charge

though no force was used,

we met.

You play your game,

and there's only one of two outcomes:

win or lose.

You throw caution to the wind,

play without a plan.

you lose.

You want to be rescued,

but first you must be in danger.

I lose.

### III

Just when I thought the test was over

and demonic insomnia was gone,

a new round starts

anxiety penetrating deep.

It's been a week.

I've had this feeling before

but this time seems different

it looks like it's here to stay.

state of worry, burrowing inside,

leaving nothing unturned,

soft underbelly, vulnerable points exposed

The violent emotions of love, its bitter-sweetness,

insatiable hunger

tension pushing to the edge

contrary to what we thought

love was.

When the dust settles

imaginary resolution in the air

but little is resolved, the sore points remain

fuel for future shows.

It was all so unreal, and yet I believed it

that luck had brought us together

and it would remain so forever and ever

but life had other plans

insisted that everything had an ending.

Time is a stingy bitch.

It limits everyone else's existence,

puts no limit on itself.

So, we separate

but it can't be the end,

just an interval on the way to perfection.

### IV

The face in the mirror peering at the horizon,

ignores what's within reach for what's far,

what's present for what's missing.

It looks away when it should look within.


The face in the mirror looks like me

but it isn't my face.


The face in the mirror looks like you

and it is your face,

the bias of mirrors.


I look at your face, as you stand in front of me

then I look at your face in the mirror,

different ways of being you.

The idols of yesteryear, half-forgotten

show up again after long disappearance.

They were once close to reality

and now they're here, shining in the mirror.

Half-forgotten isn't forgotten.

# Unconscious

Now that I look back at things

I know what happened.

It was the pride and pleading in her eyes

That confused me

Canceled each other.

That's why I did nothing.

I couldn't take it just because it was there.

Fear and favor at the same moment

distorted perceptions, frayed nerves

source without resource

I couldn't take it, so I left.

# Picture Incomplete

Rummaging through a drawer full of old receipts, expired invitations, birthday cards,

leftovers from a previous era

evidence of time that slipped away.

Although all of the items had something to do with me,

it felt like they weren't mine,

that I was thieving through someone else's belongings.

Time creating distance, dispossession.


Spending hours sifting through old papers, scribblings,

searching for a note from way back, a particular phrase

which is at the tip of my pen but escapes expression,

I can't find it in my drawer.

I can't nail it in my brain.

It's somewhere in my memory.

I'd give anything to see it.


Searching for too long

hardly showing results

the point of decision

can't be delayed any longer.

Unable to face this reality

I appeal to imagination

for showing the way, anyway.

Searching some more, failing to complete the picture

the project remains incomplete,

the gap remains,

leaving too much to the imagination.

Going through the same thing

twice,

though what I did was not the same

ended up in the same place.

# What I See and Don't See

It's early in the morning, things are foggy but I see clearly

what's in front of me, who's with me,

when victory seemed at hand, the calculus changed,

everything changed, just thinking about it hurts

but the subject is unavoidable.

We missed the moment when retreat was possible.

Now we're in the thick of it, fumbling through.


Things are foggy but I see clearly

what's in front of me, who's with me.

You can neither save me, nor can I save you.

Together into our separate destinies.


I see the road maintenance crew, Toyota car dealership, Chateau
d'Antoinette, not really a chateau but a government subsidized
housing project, the fancy sounding French name probably
chosen to mock the poor residents under the guise of elevating
their status.

A river without a name.

Turning right, the dome visible from a distance,

dominating the landscape.

Farther ahead, the Vets Hospital on a hill (are all vet hospitals
built on a hill)?

Familiar buildings and scenes.

I'm almost there.

Will start with filling the gaps,

making sure that love finds a home.


Reading the signs correctly,

neglect's damage.

Stocking the energy to resurrect the self,

to pull it out of the mean swamp of contraries.

Not just saying, but doing.


Although we know, we pretend we don't know,

thinking it's easier that way.

Instead of challenging and confronting, we let go.

But it doesn't go.

# Links

The world cannot accommodate you.

Neither fight nor flight will save you.

You have to face what you have to face.

Among your mistakes:

Throwing seeds onto a soil not ready to receive it,

wrong rhythm for the right rhyme.

The object is not objective.

It depends on who sees it, how you see it.

At the moment of transgression

you seemed so calm and focused

in the midst of much turmoil


Some sequences are linked, one way or another,

how things are, how they should be.

The yes and no of the wrecking ball before construction,

the lingering feeling of unease after pleasure,

the hurt of passion in the dead of the night,

the shame of trauma in the eyes of the beloved.

the right place for the I in love.

Some blessings arrive only in disguise.

# Empty Circle

Draw an empty circle.

Imagine all the things you don't want,

all the things making your life miserable.

Drop them there and walk away.

If you hear them calling you, don't reply.

Ignore them. Leave them there.

# Is Seeing Believing?

Seeing is believing,

I've heard it said so many times

but we see what we want to see,

so believing is also seeing.


It's confusing.


Seeing and believing depend on us

what we want.

Sentiments, intuitions, needs, challenge the sovereign mind

spreading disorder.

On the verge of being overwhelmed,

mind ready to speak itself, seeing and believing, the disorder at
the center:

reasoning wheels begin to stir,

too slow to catch up with wants and needs.

# If There's a Chance

If there's a chance to move to a different space

where the hours pass less quickly

though earth is the same, the cycle is the same;

the orderly sequence of day and night

in stark contrast with the disorder inside

defying mitigation or explanation

knowing very well that the season of miracles is over

and everyone is on his own.


A wild river at odds with its banks.

Time flowing so quickly, we don't know where it's going

and no chance to retrieve it.

It's a wild chase through minefields

and only the lucky and foolish survive,

so why rush to join?


If there's a chance for a different pace

it would have to be invented

at another time, beyond time,

there's your chance.

# Knowing How to Fail

She passed the building and was waiting for the light to change

so she could cross the street.

Something seized her, and she turned her head and looked back

and upward, as if she remembered to note how tall was the

building.

It was done so automatically, so unconsciously,

as if an invisible force compelled her to look back,

to make this building stand out in her mind before the looming

encounter.


Heedless of the many arguments to dissuade her

some of them her own,

she pushed on

to confront him at the edge.

It felt right that way,

a make or break moment.


Standing straight and poised, she delivered

what she promised herself,

the message registered.

But then what?

Wait for the counter move?

Move on?

Repeat the tried and failed methods

perpetuating the cold hell of despair.


For her, the past is the past.

She doesn't dwell on it.

And when it visits her, she may oblige

whether it comes in the shape of an angel or monster,

she handles it the best way she can.

She failed so many times,

she's become an expert in failure;

still, she often gets her way,

gets what she wants.

I didn't know why.


I thought and thought about it

found no answer.

Then one day, it all became clear:

She knows how to fail

That's why, that's why she succeeds.

# Incomplete Picture

I hear the sound but what does it mean?

An urgent reminder,

a slip in judgment or failure of the imagination

the words beating in my throat won't come out,

leaving the dots unconnected.


Facing the same results

though the acts were not the same.

Why?

Knowing the answer won't solve the problem

of dots that don't connect.

Could make it easier to bear

till the next round.


The picture that emerges is not what you expect.

Distorted, incomplete.


It's not what you think.

Sequence out of order.

Dangled phrases.

It's not what you want.


Errant Image zooms through,

settles in my eyes,

adding to the disturbance

destabilizing the unstable

and feeling at home.

# Doing with nothing.

Time for a break from the pleadings,

The exhortations, the colorless, tasteless noise.

Time for living, not as someone says

you should, but as you want.

No points, lectures or lessons,

Just living.


You dig into your fading memories

Looking for the key to the disorder

You find nothing.


It's not just rhetoric.

You know the moment of reckoning is soon

And you'll have to do with nothing.

# Your Dilemma

Why are things the way they are, you ask.

I have no explanation.

You tell me

What it will take to right things

And you will see further than your eyes can see.


You waited for so long.

Your day has come.

The waiting is over.

Out of the cave, you come,

to the darkness outside

an unwelcome guest of the night.

# Why We Can't Stop

I'm not done

don't want to stop.

She wants to stop.


She is not done

don't want to stop.

I want to stop.


We pass each other

like this,

so we never stop.

# You & I

Some days you're giving,

I can deal with that.

Other days you hold back,

I can deal with that.

Some days you give and hold back,

Don't know what to make of that.

Disagreements, conflicts, are all part of it.

You are who you are, your past is your past.

You can't just snap your finger

wipe the slate clean

re-write everything.

There will always be a residue pointing to events, time, places,

to the marks on body and mind.

So, when I saw you had that glow

I wanted you so much, not the image from memory

but the real thing, in all its fading glory.

# This Thing

In the distance a flag perched at the peak of the dome

not far away from the tower,

pale light announcing a new day

the drumbeat of time slipping away,

heart exposed, telling a convoluted story

half-forgotten, half-dreamt

the part that matters.

Can't be saved by mastery

gained through treachery

the adultery of words,

mere promises

can't quench the thirst

nor drive away this crazy insistence,

this thing,

raising questions

for which I have no answer

making all efforts seem in vain.


Drifting on a pitiful boat, the sea getting wider,

The sky closer

So much emptiness above the sea

So much life below it.

A couple of waves strike the boat

Almost capsize it

Driving away the urge to venture or adventure.

# Joy

Things were looking doubtful

or so I believed, then a jolt;

joy arrived out of nowhere,

it doesn't matter that it wasn't planned,

that I'm not the one who made it happen.

Joy is joy, should be enjoyed.

# Price of Change

The ecstasy of the hunt,

the illusion of solitude,

no longer matter.

A project that lost its thrill.


The past should be the past

but it's re-born,

taking us in its grip.


Why so much focus on moments of glory

or escape into solitude

when they only deepen the hurt?

It's crazy to re-birth the past or re-live it

but what's the alternative? Live without memory?


The sadness of the blue sky

as it gives up its blue-ness,

threads of white and gray clouds

a new scene takes shape

slowly but surely

making its presence felt;

everything has a downside

the price that must be paid

to make that movement

from state to state, stage to stage.

# Hardly Working

Yesterday, I worked till late at night

but the task still not finished.

Started today where I left.

Hours have passed and I'm still at it.

Quit or continue

What should I do?


I want to end this uncertainty,

stand on solid ground

instead, things get shakier.


This isn't working.

Let me try again.


One more day at work,

little progress,

the ugly gap

between wishes and reality,

fragments of insights, loads of frustration

what ifs,

a sea of regrets.

# Ends and Means

Investing time and energy to persuade, convince,

using different tools, benefits and profits

setting body against mind

sophistry, underhanded trickery,

the patient, insistent geometric progression of evil

the degraded satisfaction of being an object of attention.

You call that success, but is it?

# Self – Exposed

Doing away with protocol and niceties,

Like mad wind ripping the elaborate mask

Exposing abandoned dreams

Overtaken by fears and worries

Debts that must be settled

Self, alone, not knowing its place

The last jewel gambled.

You thought your task was clear: to pull yourself

Out of the acrid swamp of self-repetition

Back to the fresh air of rolling fields.

That didn't happen.

Now you have to make a decision.

It was easier to fail, so you took that route

And you're still paying for it.

Telescoping the moment, through the right angle

Closing in on its history, identifying winners and losers

The unwritten rules of the game

Depravity of the dividing hour

Splitting the psyche

No wonder happiness is so hard?


Every action pulled down by previous inaction,

duty abdicating to doubt, challenged by

the path of difference,

how to restore movement,

belief in a questionable future.

# Work

This feeling of being so close to the work, so utterly alone with
it, is hard to explain.

Part of you wants to keep it that way

another part wants to end it.


Mind says time to trade for lighter things.

Heart says it feels so good, it hurts.

Another version of the cliché art in suffering.


Throw one more log in the fireplace,

comforting warmth of light and cracking sound

flame and wood locked, close at work.

Does it really hurt, pain in pleasure,

until all turns to ashes?


Stepping outside, morning spreads its wings little by little.

Waiting for spring, for the clothes and air to be lighter.

I will soon be downtown:

skyscrapers, cars, workers, thugs, everyone in a hurry,

the crowd becomes one, assimilating everyone.

I become part of them.

Cold air saved for two seasons, then released

past the point I can bear

waiting for spring, for the shedding of skin,

the miracle of warmth

until then, a few rays of light will do.

# Personal History Transformed

Need when expressed is no longer need.

It's a state revealed

obliges us to attend to the matter,

before it transforms to an unpredictable state.


The moment when each is himself, not the sum

of different parts.

When we look back and make our own histories

and believe in it, because we made it

and only we can claim it,

it's ours, a singular achievement

and we've learned a thing or two,

escaped the trap of using the plural for personal ends.

# Catalogue of Obstacles

The things holding me back:

Reaction, not action.

Escape from, not to.

The tricks I play on myself:

Temporary relief perpetuating the malady

hopping from somewhere to nowhere.


I know the drill,

long stretches of confusion, doubts and questioning,

then moments of lucidity, things become clear.

The cycle repeats itself.

I want to step into the cycle, break it open,

mold it into a different shape,

put an end to endless repetition,

let being float.


I want to clear the things weighing on me

what's the relation between me and you,

between me and me, between you and you?

How to overcome this obstacle of me and you?

I turned to you for help.

Looking at it from different angles

changing style, not substance

turning things to your advantage.

A master manipulator of the night

making sure you're seen in the best light.

# Thought & Style

Thought crosses the mind

and with it the urge to translate,

to reflect into reality,

extinguishing pure thought.


When the primary color of thoughts

matches desire

the emerging picture appealing

to action.

To make what was thought and desired

a reality.


To do things with style.

To do them with flair

expertise and ease,

keep the balance between subject and object

the stylistics of being.

Sometimes it means just to have the wherewithal

such as saying to travel in style, meaning to travel in comfort

and many of your needs taken care of.

All of that, is commonly known, but it misses the point.

Style can't be defined. It can only be described.

It's a particular way of being

from the way you dress, relate, eat, walk, talk

what makes you you and not someone else.

# Un-learned Lesson

Barreling down a river of trouble full speed,

no time to evaluate the unfolding scenario

no time to escape or think of stratagems.

Raiding the inner sanctum and coming out empty

dizzying effect of the let down

grasping straws to prevent the downward spiral

but it's happening, the race to the bottom.

No way out.

One of the lessons learned, not to repeat the same mistake

but the mistake is repeated.

Which says the lesson was not learned or was un-learned

mistake on the verge of crime.

# Why I Hold Back

Amazing was the spectacle

but one round is enough for now.

Have to economize on a good thing,

save it for other occasions

when it will be much needed.


If you wonder where the calculation to save and defer comes

from,

it come from several places,

foremost, knowing what's special doesn't take place often

plus, the fear of addiction to what can only be rarely obtained.

Convergence of these factors and others

Make me hold back.

# Missed Opportunities

I went up the street then made a U turn

to check on the queen of green smiles.

She was there as usual, happy to see me.

We exchanged greetings, asked me where I had been

and blessed me.


The last time I held you, I thought I won't see you again

though I felt I will see you again.

It's always the discrepancy between thought and feeling

that fixes a vice grip on me, vitiating my strength

so that when I go, I leave nothing behind,

everything as neat and predictable as a dog lolling its tongue.


I went to the right place at the wrong time

and the wrong place at the right time,

left a trail of missed opportunities everyone could see

except me,

because I lacked something called strategic patience,

waiting for something that wasn't there

that may or may not happen.

This is hard for me, harder than learning a foreign language.

# Cat and Mouse

A cat scampering back and forth on the stairs

playing cat and mouse with itself,

a gratuitous activity, doing something for nothing, for its own

sake, the unexplored nothing that refuses to be quantified,

measured, assessed.

You enjoy doing it, you feel pleased.

Or you please others,

you like that feeling,

so you do it again, or, whenever possible.

Sometimes at an inappropriate time

And although you enjoyed it, joy is mixed with guilt,

Not because you did it but because you did it at the wrong place

or time.

# Chewing Leftovers

Last night we talked,

covered a lot of territory,

had the best conversation in a long time.

It wasn't easy, went through a lot of hurdles

chewed the leftovers of hurtful events, words

tasting even more bitter.

Time only makes these kinds of things worse.

We neither skirted the overgrown pain nor dwelled on it

just dealt with it as it came,

not treating it as specimen to be sent to a lab, examined under a

microscope.

Let the agreements, disagreements take their course,

the blood pressure rise and fall.

Stepping back, allowing a different reality to unfold.

# It Could've Been

The place to be

where you're wanted

not Where you're unwanted

is the place to be.

That was what she said to me.

As I thought about it,

trying to explain to myself what she said;

that she knew when she was valued, made to feel at home,

and when she was not welcome,

but this is just repeating what she said,

not explaining it.

So, what did she mean?

I don't know.

I'm not sure.

It could be that she was grandstanding,

telling me she knew things I didn't know.

It could have been a warning for me to shape up, telling me

she's reaching her limit.

It could have been a breakup notice,

saying goodbye in a convoluted way:

the place to be is

where you're wanted

# About Stories and Other Things

Stories told and re-told, fact and fiction,

no matter,

draining the emotions,

the day just started and it's already late and old

despite the new garb.

Will watch it go by, too,

neither blessing nor cursing,

just another day,

ending as it began, late and old.

It's like something at the tip of the tongue

but isn't there when you need it

arrives late, and instead of helping becomes a burden

you want to un-do it, remove it from your

consciousness, so you can move to other things.

Waiting for more info to make the decision,

empty the mind and chest of words, events, objects,

things that occupy space but do not coalesce into a whole,

the info arrives but still no decision;

Actually, the information was always there

but the will wasn't.


An errant instance it was,

could've been good or bad,

we'll never know cause

could've been can't be known.

Waiting for the light to change at the intersection,

a Toyota hits a Harley Davidson sending it crashing

on the curb. As the biker tried to get up,

lips cut, skin torn off his knees and arms

screaming, "God damn. Fuck this. Shit. I've just bought it, it's new, it's new."

Said nothing about his bleeding knees and torn skin.

Good news arrived,

but the one person who mattered,

the one I wanted to share this blessing

wasn't here.

And I can't enjoy it alone.

Don't know how.

Heard the story ten times

but every time it seems new,

history in motion, transformed in action.

The secret of a good story isn't in the tables,

profiles of losses and gains, but in the telling.


You see what time has done, is doing

You feel it, live it.

See yourself, see others,

the cycle repeats itself

until the moment of altered consciousness

You see yourself in others.


Starting is the hardest.

We think we need to know so much before we start

so we never start.

Let's start with what we know

Or, if you think it's too little

let's begin with a question.

The little you know and the question you ask

will point you towards possibilities you had not entertained

places you had never been.

The questions every story must answer:

Where is the story headed?

What stops does it make?

Where is it coming from?

How does it upset the applecart?

History hinting its meaning only in action.

Not what's left behind, the leftovers, but what's here.

Making present happenings.

In the asymmetry between what is, what was, what will be

possibility emerges, though nothing is guaranteed

whether it ends in climax or anti-climax

it's our story, one of many.

I wanted to think of it

as just a story among stories

of rising and falling

pleasure and pain

a linear path of days and nights.

Love knows its home and how to get there

But to get there, has to overcome obstacles,

stop worrying about what may happen once it gets there.

That's another story.

You ask for the whole story

but the story is not whole.

Loose ends blown by the wind

in different directions,

seeds for new stories

Waiting for the dust to settle

the view is dimmer

a half-full cup on the table,

focus on the present half

or the missing half?

Waiting for the view to get clearer.

Energized by the sun and breeze

stepping on sand, pebbles, and rocks

salty taste in my mouth

the old sensations are back

but I can't afford them.

Their toll too high.

# The Last Game

The line running from the bridge of your nose

down your lips

attracting immediate undivided attention

linking motion and emotion.

A miniature of you.

I'm ready for another round.

The expressions on your face

say so many things.

Inviting and rejecting in the same breath

adding to the uncertainty,

weakening the resolve

to go with you all the way

submit to the disorder.


This is the last game.

The playing field is not level.

There're a dozen ways for me to lose

and one way to win.

This isn't what I wanted, or, where I wanted to be

but we are where we are.

Action is the master and words have to give way.


It's the last game.

It's stacked in your favor.

I'm just a player.

It's your game.

Printed in the United States
by Baker & Taylor Publisher Services